Self-esteem
Therapy

Self~esteem Therapy

written by
Karen Katafiasz

illustrated by
R.W. Alley

A ONE
CARING
PLACE

Abbey Press

Text © 1995 Karen Katafiasz
Illustrations © 1995 St. Meinrad Archabbey
Published by One Caring Place
Abbey Press
St. Meinrad, Indiana 47577

Library of Congress Catalog Number
95-79515

ISBN 0-87029-280-3

Printed in the United States of America

Foreword

Some people spend all their lives refusing to face an emptiness within them, a void that communicates an aching sense of wrongness and shame about themselves.

They may try to cover the pain with material success and accomplishments, or numb it with unhealthy behavior, or turn to others to fill up this "hole in the soul," as John Bradshaw calls it.

What they lack is self-esteem.

Self-esteem is more than feeling self-confident or spouting positive affirmations. It goes to the heart of personal identity, conveying the belief that we are acceptable, respected, and loved as the persons we are—with all our feelings and sensations and even imperfections.

The source of self-esteem lies deep within childhood, from the first moment a vulnerable infant seeks to get its needs met from a caregiving adult. These needs go beyond physical nourishment and safety. To thrive, a child must be acknowledged, accepted, loved without condition. That's an agenda even the most well-intentioned parent can't always accommodate.

The good news is that, as an adult, you have power to change an inner sense of wrongness, to fill an emptiness within. With reassuring insight, *Self-esteem Therapy* invites you to go deep within to heal your wounded self-esteem. Make an appointment today for some *Self-esteem Therapy!*

1.

Know the reality of your worth as a wondrous, one-of-a-kind, loved, and lovable child of God. You make a dent in creation that cannot be duplicated. That is the basis of self-esteem. No one and nothing can take that reality from you.

2.

Self-esteem is more than an air of self-confidence, a superior attitude, positive messages playing on your inner tape, or a jaunty strut through the world. It's being truly at ease and at peace with yourself. It's the knowledge deep within that you matter and you're acceptable just as you are.

3.

Self-esteem is a solidness at
the core of your being.
Without sufficient self-esteem,
you have a painful emptiness,
a "hole in the soul" aching
to be filled. Recognize that
hollowness; only you can
fill it up.

4.

Shame destroys and displaces
self-esteem. It erodes your
spirit, carving out an emptiness
inside. It produces a heaviness
at the bottom of your being,
even as it makes you feel
hollow. Be alert to shame
lurking within you.

5.

"Healthy" shame tells you that you've done something terribly wrong. "Toxic" shame tells you that you <u>are</u> terribly wrong. You need to deal with both kinds of shame.

6.

You generate and strengthen self-esteem when you live with integrity, in harmony with your values. Consciously and thoughtfully choose meaningful principles in which to ground your life. Commit yourself to them with all your heart.

7.

When your actions violate your values, you feel "healthy" shame. To remove that feeling, admit what you've done, accept responsibility for the consequences, and make amends to anyone you've hurt. Then forgive yourself.

8.

Sometimes when you find yourself doing what you don't like, you'll have to probe beneath the surface to discover what's driving your actions. If you're acting from unmet needs, deal with them. Seek out spiritual or psychological guidance, when that's appropriate.

9.

You can use "healthy" shame to learn, to grow, to become more the person you want to be. After you take responsibility for what you did and make amends, decide what you need to do to ensure that your future actions will be in harmony with your principles.

10.

Just as doing good things builds self-esteem, so does doing things well. Recognize where you shine, and share that glow with the universe.

11.

Reflect on those moments when you've felt good about yourself. Reexperience the sense of strength, self-acceptance, and serenity that filled your being. When your self-esteem is shaky, you can tap into the wellspring of these emotional memories, letting the feelings flow through you once more.

12.

Keep challenging yourself to grow, even when that means you could fail. View your mistakes as occasions for learning—not occasions for shame—on the way to becoming all that you're meant to be.

13.

Imagine self-esteem as a ray of energy, vibrating from your feet to the top of your head. It anchors you in a solid appreciation of who you are right now, at the same time it keeps pulling you upward toward higher aspirations— upward to the stars.

14.

The emptiness and sense of wrongness that come with low self-esteem can be unbearably painful. Work to build up self-esteem in healthy ways and remove shame at its source. If you don't, you may use harmful, self-defeating ways to feel better.

15.

Don't try to fill your inner emptiness or numb your pain with mood-altering substances or behavior. Though you may seem to feel better at first, these are phony, short-lived "solutions" and will eventually send what self-esteem you do have spiraling even lower.

16.

Material success and accomplishments may distract you for a time, but they won't give you real self-esteem or remove your pain. You need to face the emptiness that lies within.

17.

Depending on other people's approval to make you feel better about yourself is like an addiction. This will work for a time, but you'll have to keep pursuing their acceptance again and again. You'll lose yourself in the process. The approval you need is your own.

18.

You may try to feel better about yourself by criticizing and attacking others and being competitive with them. Stop. This will only exhaust you and fill you with bitterness.

19.

You may try to get rid of your feelings of shame by projecting them onto others. But shame will only replenish itself within you. Recognize when you're shaming others in an attempt to give away your own shame.

20.

Be aware when "toxic" shame sends the message not that you made a mistake but that you are a mistake. Toxic shame is as deadly to your spirit as a toxic chemical is to your body. Pledge to rid yourself of it.

21.

Toxic shame can be like an archeological site, with layers of shaming messages that have accumulated over the years. To unearth the "you" at the very bottom takes patience, hard work, and care-full scrutiny of the contents of each layer. It's worth it.

22.

To develop self-esteem, you needed—as you were growing up—loving, caring nurturing that affirmed your worth, mirroring back to you your God-given dignity and value. Remember the nurturing you received, and cherish those who provided it for you.

23.

If you grew to adulthood with damaged self-esteem, it's because you received messages about yourself that were distorted and shaming or you didn't receive enough positive messages that affirmed your worth. You now have the power and responsibility to heal your wounded self-esteem.

24.

When you ache with a sense of "wrongness" about yourself, when you realize you're ashamed to be you, take time to explore what's going on. What are you hearing in the deepest part of yourself? You can change the message.

25.

If significant persons in your childhood neglected, rejected, or abused you or used shame to discipline you, you probably assumed that you were bad, unworthy, and inadequate. Mourn for what was done to you. Then determine whether those beliefs still reverberate within; contradict them with the truth.

26.

Prejudice and ignorance can produce cultural messages that shame you and assault your self-esteem, suggesting that you look wrong or have the wrong heritage or religion or don't measure up in some way. If you've internalized these messages, root them out.

27.

Many shaming messages in our society are about the body and bodily functions. Examine the shame you feel surrounding your body. Replace this shame with an appreciation for the amazing masterpiece that God has created.

28.

When others attempt to
shame you, they may act
out of a pattern they use in a
desperate—and futile—attempt
to feel better about themselves.
And you may respond out of
your own pattern of accepting
the shame they offer. They may
not change their pattern; you
can change yours.

29.

Don't get stuck in blaming those who've shamed you and damaged your self-esteem; that keeps you their victim. Instead, reject what they've done and realize that their messages to you reflect their own shame and low self-esteem, not the reality of who you are.

30.

If you were used to being
shamed as a child, you may feel
that's what's happening when
others criticize you. Separate
constructive criticism from
messages of shame.

31.

When you are being shamed, anger is a healthy reaction, because it means that you don't accept what's being done to you. Express your anger in safe, constructive, and respectful ways.

32.

Hold people accountable for their actions without shaming them. Let them know when their behavior hurts you and why. Suggest behavior that is more respectful of you and recognizes your rights.

33.

Though other people can't hand you self-esteem, they can support you and offer the kind of positive messages that you need to hear and believe. Seek out friends who recognize your goodness and who lovingly affirm your worth.

34.

Give up shame as a way of life.
Without shame, you have the
freedom to just be you—the
unique, delightful person that
God imagined into being.

35.

Live from your center. That is where God is whispering: "I am always with you; you are mine."

Karen Katafiasz is a writer and editor. She is the author of *Finding Your Way Through Grief, Celebrate-your-womanhood Therapy, Grief Therapy,* and *Christmas Therapy.* A native of Toledo, Ohio, she now lives in Santa Claus, Indiana.

Illustrator for the Abbey Press Elf-help Books, **R.W. Alley** also illustrates and writes children's books. He lives in Barrington, Rhode Island, with his wife, daughter, and son.

The Story of the Abbey Press Elves

The engaging figures that populate the Abbey Press "elf-help" line of publications and products first appeared in 1987 on the pages of a small self-help book called *Be-good-to-yourself Therapy*. Shaped by the publishing staff's vision and defined in R.W. Alley's inventive illustrations, they lived out author Cherry Hartman's gentle, self-nurturing advice with charm, poignancy, and humor.

Reader response was so enthusiastic that more Elf-help Books were soon under way, a still-growing series that has inspired a line of related gift products.

The especially endearing character featured in the early books—sporting a cap with a mood-changing candle in its peak—has since been joined by a spirited female elf with flowers in her hair.

These two exuberant, sensitive, resourceful, kindhearted, lovable sprites, along with their lively elfin community, reveal what's truly important as they offer messages of joy and wonder, playfulness and co-creation, wholeness and serenity, the miracle of life and the mystery of God's love.

With wisdom and whimsy, these little creatures with long noses demonstrate the elf-help way to a rich and fulfilling life.

Elf-help Books

...adding "a little character" and a lot
of help to self-help reading!

Elf-help for Healing from Divorce	#20082
Music Therapy	#20083
Elf-help for a Happy Retirement	#20085
'Tis a Blessing to Be Irish	#20088
Getting Older, Growing Wiser	#20089
Worry Therapy	#20093
Elf-help for Raising a Teen	#20102
Elf-help for Being a Good Parent	#20103
Gratitude Therapy	#20105
Garden Therapy	#20116
Elf-help for Busy Moms	#20117
Trust-in-God Therapy	#20119
Elf-help for Overcoming Depression	#20134
New Baby Therapy	#20140
Grief Therapy for Men	#20141
Living From Your Soul	#20146

Acceptance Therapy (color edition) $5.95	#20182
Acceptance Therapy	#20190
Keeping-up-your-spirits Therapy	#20195
Play Therapy	#20200
Slow-down Therapy	#20203
One-day-at-a-time Therapy	#20204
Prayer Therapy	#20206
Be-good-to-your-marriage Therapy	#20205
Be-good-to-yourself Therapy (hardcover) $10.95	#20196
Be-good-to-yourself Therapy	#20255

Book price is $4.95 unless otherwise noted.
Available at your favorite giftshop or bookstore—
or directly from One Caring Place, Abbey Press
Publications, St. Meinrad, IN 47577.
Or call 1-800-325-2511.